The 4 Cuties - Freundinnen
Extra Diamond Edition
english

For my husband

Author / images / Cover:

Tanja M. Feiler

Content

I. The Cutiesong

The 4 Cuties
are the best
friends yes
they running in the land
hand in hand
hand in hand
running in the land
the 4 cuties are the best

2. Lyrics

The diamonds shining bright
in the light
they have a great
collection of pics
with one click

Freundinnen - that is the
expression of their
confession

more and more

they are four

4 - that is the number

does it mean fun there?

Yes of course

that is the force

the collectiv

the cuties

The girls are specialists

therapists

and making reports

about make - up and

sports

for that

what

is amazing and brings good

feelings

3. Gallery

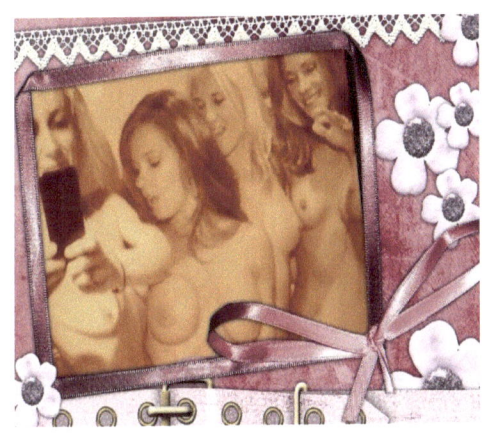

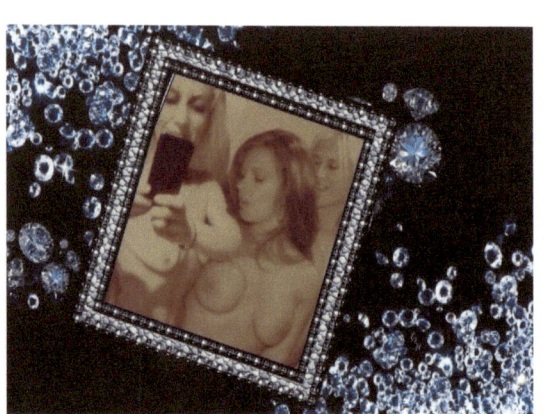

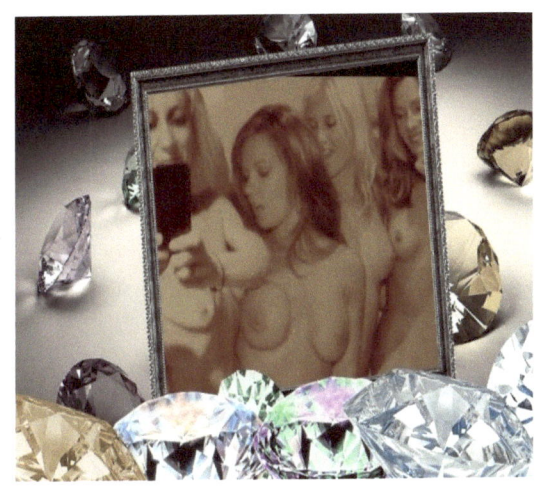

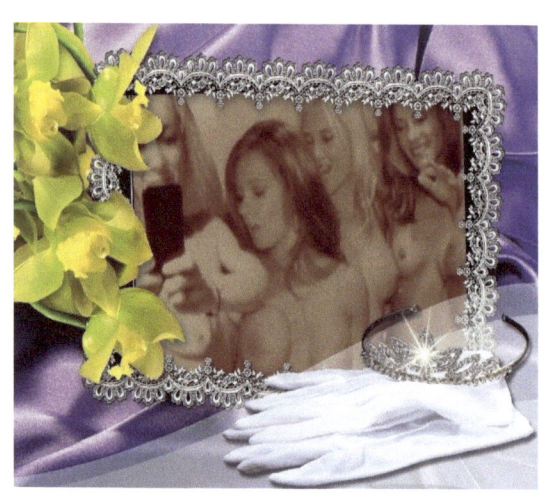

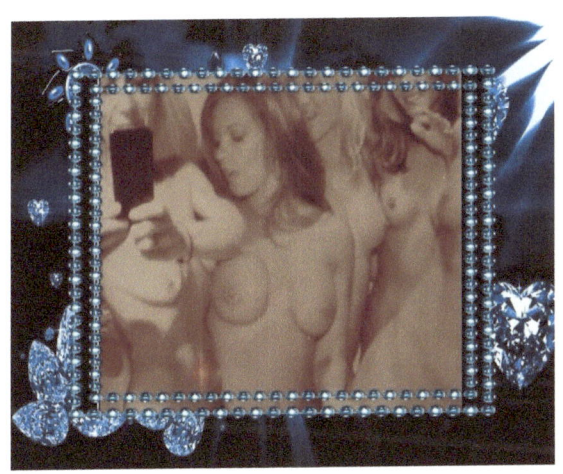

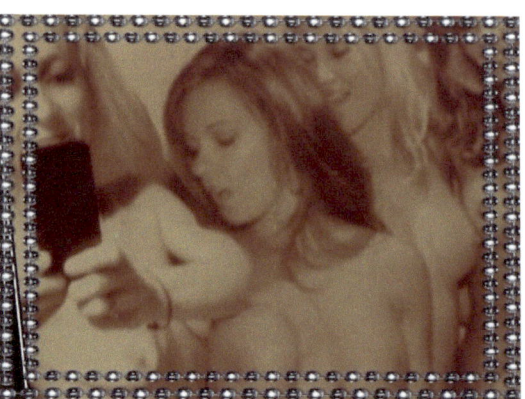

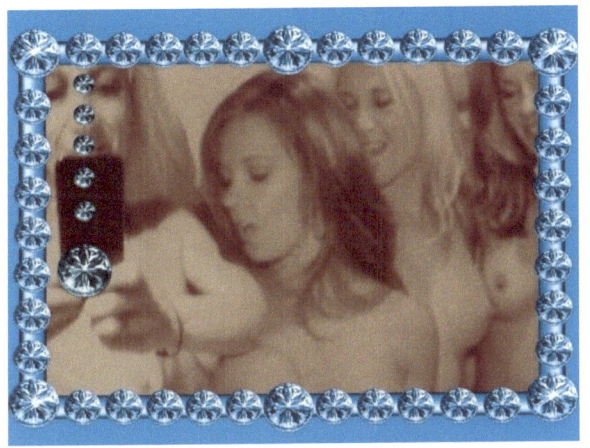

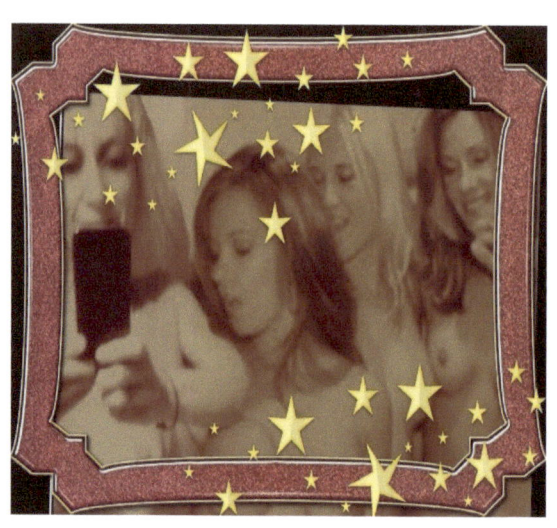

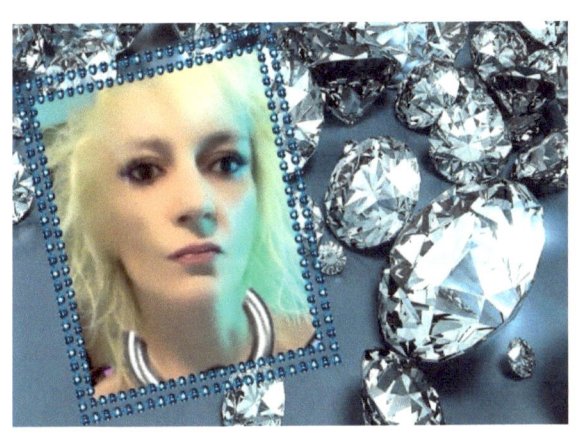

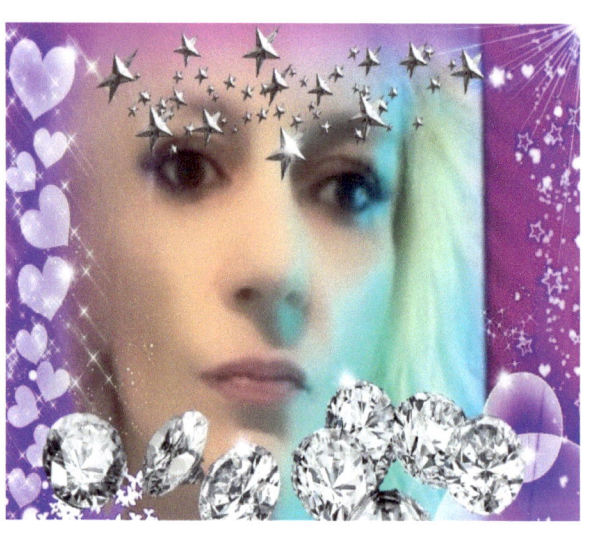

Sing the song all time long

with the girls they are the best

all come together

for a better

understanding

The 4 Cuties are in the land

going hand in hand

finding the right way

every day

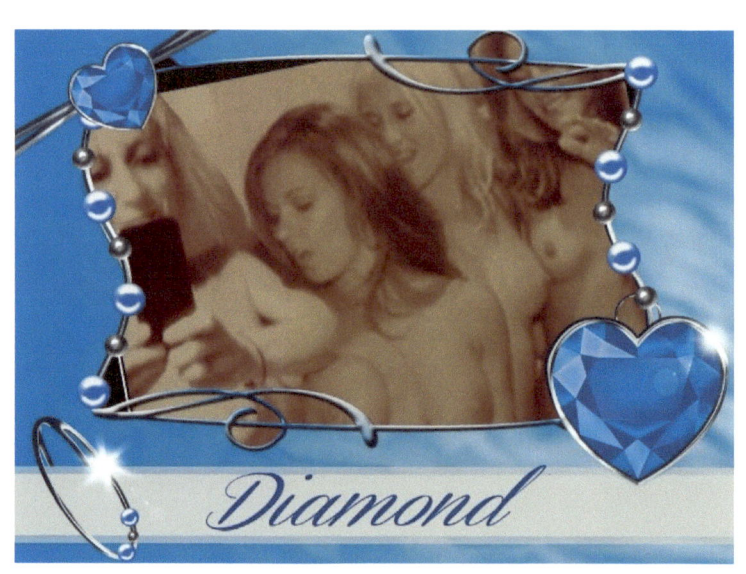

Diamond

Especially I say Thank you
to my husband

www.ingramcontent.com/pod-product-compliance
Lightning Source LLC
Chambersburg PA
CBHW041622180526
45159CB00002BC/980